UNCLE GRANDPA

CHEESY Joke Book

HUG Me

BY WRIGLEY STUART

CARTOON NETWORK BOOKS

An Imprint of Penguin Random House

HEY,
I MADE UP ALL THESE
JOKES MYSELF. REALLY. THESE
RIDDLES AREN'T JUST COOL,
THEY'RE FREEZING COLD, WHICH
IS, LIKE, EXTRA COOL, IF YOU
THINK ABOUT IT.

CARTOON NETWORK BOOKS
Penguin Young Readers Group
An Imprint of Penguin Random House LLC

Penguin supports copyright. Copyright fuels creativity, encourages diverse voices, promotes free speech, and creates a vibrant culture. Thank you for buying an authorized edition of this book and for complying with copyright laws by not reproducing, scanning, or distributing any part of it in any form without permission. You are supporting writers and allowing Penguin to continue to publish books for every reader.

ISBN 978-0-8431-8347-4

10 9 8 7 6 5 4 3 2 1

Pizza Steve's Coolest Jokes

What do you get when you cross
Pizza Steve with a radio?
Cool music.

Why does Pizza Steve wear frozen Band-Aids?
Because he gets cold cuts.

Why did Pizza Steve
put all his money in Uncle
Grandpa's freezer?
**'Cause he wanted
some cold cash.**

Where does
Pizza Steve keep his money?
In a snow bank.

6

How do snowmen get places?
They travel by icicle.

Where do snowmen dance?
At snow balls.

What do snowmen eat for breakfast?
Frosted Flakes.

What do you call a dinosaur
that's a noisy sleeper?
A bronto-snorus.

What do you call a dinosaur with poor eyesight?
A do-you-think-he-saw-us.

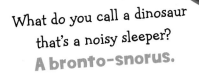

What do you call a
dinosaur with high heels?
A my-feet-are-sore-us.

What has a spiked tail, plates on
its back, and sixteen wheels?
**A stegosaurus on roller
skates.**

14

15

17

19

23

Didn't those jokes just knock you over laughing? Do you have your own knock-knock jokes you like to tell? Write them into the blanks below!

Knock, knock!
Who's there?

_____.
_____ *who?*

_____
_____
_____.

Knock, knock!
Who's there?

_____.
_____ *who?*

_____
_____
_____.

Knock, knock!
Who's there?

_____.

_____ *who?*

_____

_____.

Knock, knock!
Who's there?

_____.

_____ *who?*

_____

_____.

Knock, knock!
Who's there?

_____.

_____ *who?*

_____.

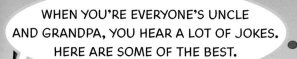

WHEN YOU'RE EVERYONE'S UNCLE AND GRANDPA, YOU HEAR A LOT OF JOKES. HERE ARE SOME OF THE BEST.

HIT ME, UNCLE G.

Uncle Grandpa's Funniest Jokes, Part 1

WHY WAS THE BROOM LATE?

I DON'T KNOW.

IT OVERSWEPT!

What happened when Mr. Gus stepped on an orange?

He hurt its peelings.

YOU SHOULDN'T TELL DIRTY JOKES, YOU KNOW.

27

What did the icy road say to Uncle Grandpa's RV?
Want to go for a spin?

How does Uncle Grandpa make an egg roll?
He pushes it.

Why did Uncle Grandpa dump ground beef on his head?

He wanted a meatier shower.

Why did Mr. Gus take a ruler to bed?

To see how long he slept.

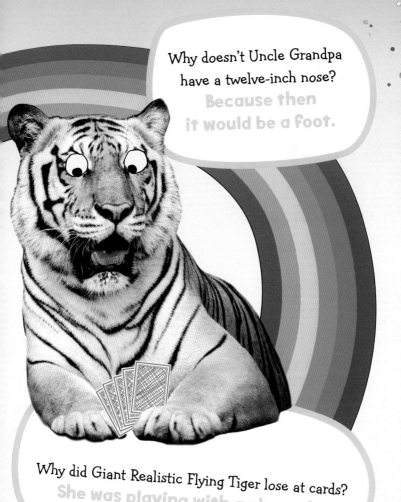

What do you call Mr. Gus on the moon?

Lost.

What did Uncle Grandpa do when he saw a space man?

He parked his car, man.

Which hand is it better for
Uncle Grandpa to write with?
Neither. It's best for him
to write with a pencil.

How many books can you put
into an empty Belly Bag?
One. After that,
Belly Bag is no longer empty.

34

What gets wetter the more it dries?
A towel.

What do you get when you cross Mr. Gus with a firecracker?
Dino-mite!

ROAR!

GIANT REALISTIC FLYING TIGER, DID YOU SAY THESE ARE YOUR FAVORITE JOKES?

Giant Realistic Flying Tiger's Favorite Jokes

ROAR!

SURE, I'D LOVE TO HEAR THEM.

ROAR!

NO, I'M NOT HUNGRY RIGHT NOW, THANKS.

Which kind of Giant Realistic Flying Dog tells time?
A Giant Realistic Flying Watchdog.

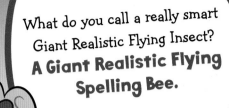

What do you call a really smart Giant Realistic Flying Insect?
A Giant Realistic Flying Spelling Bee.

What do you call a Giant Realistic Flying Fish with no eyes?
A Gant Realstc Flyng Fsh.

What's black and white and bouncy?
A Giant Realistic Flying Zebra on a pogo stick.

What do you get when you cross a yellow Giant Realistic Flying Dog with a telephone?
A Giant Realistic Flying Golden Receiver.

How did the Giant Realistic Flying Pig write a letter?
With its Giant Realistic Flying Pig Pen.

Where do Giant Realistic Flying Bugs go shopping?
At the Giant Realistic Flying Flea Market.

How do Giant Realistic Flying Frogs see at night? **With Giant Realistic Flying Frog Lights.**

How do you stop a Giant Realistic Flying Rhinoceros from charging? **Take away his Giant Realistic Flying Credit Card.**

What do you get when you cross a Giant Realistic Flying Parrot and a centipede? **A Giant Realistic Flying Walkie-Talkie.**

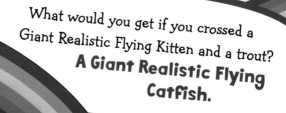

What would you get if you crossed a Giant Realistic Flying Kitten and a trout?
A Giant Realistic Flying Catfish.

What did the Giant Realistic Flying Firefly have to eat?
A Giant Realistic Flying Light Lunch.

What do you call a Giant Realistic Flying Pig that knows karate?
A Giant Realistic Flying Pork Chop.

What kind of a bone can't a
Giant Realistic Flying Dog eat?
A Giant Realistic Flying Trombone.

MR. GUS, I'M NOT SAYING YOU'RE OLD, BUT WHEN YOU WERE A KID, YOU HAD A PET DINOSAUR! HA!

I AM A DINOSAUR.

RIGHT, SO YOU HAD YOURSELF AS A PET OR SOMETHING.

Mr. Gus is so old, his memories are in black and white.

44

Mr. Gus is so old, he walked into an antiques store and they sold him.

Mr. Gus is so old that in school, history class was called "yesterday."

Mr. Gus is so old, his birth certificate expired.

Mr. Gus is so old that when he lights his birthday candles, the fire department is on standby.

Mr. Gus is so old, his Social Security number is 1.

I DON'T THINK THOSE ARE VERY FUNNY.

RELAX, BIG GUY. I'M JUST HAVING SOME FUN WITH YOU.

Mr. Gus is so old, when Pizza Steve told him to act his age, he wrapped himself up like a mummy.

47

Those Uncle Gus jokes were SO old . . . they must have come from the Old Stone Age! Write your own "Mr. Gus is so old . . ." jokes in the blanks below!

Mr. Gus is so old,

_____

_____

Mr. Gus is so old,

_____

_____

Mr. Gus is so old,
_____
_____
_____

Mr. Gus is so old,
_____
_____
_____
_____

Mr. Gus is so old,
_____
_____

HERE ARE MY ALL-TIME FAVORITE PIZZA JOKES.

Pizza Steve's Pizza Jokes

DO YOU KNOW WHY PIZZAS SHOULDN'T TELL JOKES? BECAUSE THEY'RE REALLY CHEESY.

I'M GOING TO PRETEND I DIDN'T HEAR THAT.

How do you fix a broken pizza?
With tomato paste.

53

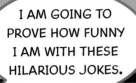

What's the difference between a guitar and a fish? Guitars have strings.

Why do bananas have to put on sunscreen before they go to the beach?
So they don't get sunburned.

What do you call a fly with no wings?
A walk.

Why do elephants have wrinkles?
Ever tried to iron an elephant?

What kind of rocks can
Uncle Grandpa never find in the ocean?
Dry ones.

Why did the bubble gum cross the road?
**Because it was stuck
to the chicken's foot.**

What's red and bad for
Uncle Grandpa's teeth?
A brick.

61

What sound do porcupines
make when they kiss?
Ouch!

What does Giant Realistic Flying Tiger
use to comb her fur?
A cat-a-comb.

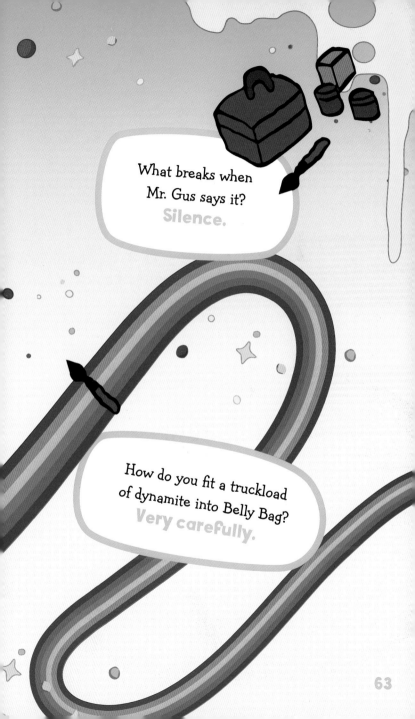

What breaks when
Mr. Gus says it?
Silence.

How do you fit a truckload
of dynamite into Belly Bag?
Very carefully.

What did the traffic light say to Uncle Grandpa's RV?

Don't look, I'm changing.

When is Uncle Grandpa's RV like a frog?

When it gets toad.

WHAT DO YOU GET WHEN YOU CROSS A POTATO WITH MR. GUS?

WHAT?

MASHED POTATOES.

Where did Uncle Grandpa take the sick boat? To the dock.

What gives milk and has one horn?
A milk truck.

What has four wheels and flies?
A garbage truck.

What did the inventor
of the door knocker win?
The no-bell prize.

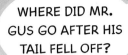

WHERE DID MR. GUS GO AFTER HIS TAIL FELL OFF?

WHERE?

Where do you find giant snails? On the ends of giants' fingers.

THE RE-TAIL STORE.

What does Mr. Gus eat?
Anything he wants.

Why did Uncle Grandpa bury his flashlight?
Because the batteries died.

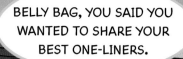

BELLY BAG, YOU SAID YOU WANTED TO SHARE YOUR BEST ONE-LINERS.

NO, I SAID THAT I NEED A NEW LINER, BECAUSE I'M A BAG. YOU KNOW, SO I DON'T LEAK.

BUT I'VE RESERVED THESE NEXT FEW PAGES FOR YOU.

Belly Bag's Favorite One-Liners

LUCKILY, I'VE GOT A BOOK OF ONE-LINERS RIGHT HERE.

If you want to catch a squirrel, just climb a tree and act like a nut.

Uncle Grandpa went to buy some camouflage trousers the other day, but he couldn't find any.

A magician was walking down the street and turned into a grocery store.

Two peanuts walked into a bar, and one was a salted.

Pizza Steve wondered why the football was getting bigger. Then it hit him.

There are three kinds of people: those who can count and those who can't.

Uncle Grandpa didn't like his haircut, but it grew on him.

Two fish are in a tank. One turns to the other and asks, "How do you drive this thing?"

Uncle Grandpa walked into a movie theater with a slab of asphalt under his arm and said, "A bag of popcorn, please, and one for the road."

Mr. Gus tried to catch fog yesterday. Mist.

Did you hear about the guy who lost the entire left side of his body in an accident? Don't worry, he's all right now.

Grandpa, Grandpa Jokes

THEY SAY LAUGHTER IS THE BEST MEDICINE. IF THAT'S TRUE, YOU CAN SAVE LOTS OF MONEY ON ASPIRIN AFTER READING THIS PART OF THE BOOK.

Grandpa, Grandpa—
I swallowed a bone.
Are you choking?
No, I really did.

Grandpa, Grandpa—
I keep forgetting things.
What was that?
What was what?

77

79

It's so hot . . .

. . . everyone is wearing sweat pants.

. . . the cows are giving evaporated milk.

. . . birds are using pot holders to pull worms out of the ground.

. . . Uncle Grandpa's clothes iron themselves.

IT'S SO HOT THAT NO ONE IS COOL ANYMORE—EXCEPT PIZZA STEVE, OF COURSE, BECAUSE I'M ALWAYS COOL.

It is so hot . . .

. . . global warming has been replaced by global melting.

. . . chickens are laying hard-boiled eggs.

. . . when Mr. Gus opened up an ear of corn, he found popcorn.

Those Pizza Steve jokes were SO hot . . . this joke book almost caught on fire! Write your own "Pizza Steve is so hot . . ." jokes in the blanks below!

Pizza Steve is SO hot . . .

. . . _____

_____

. . . _____

_____

. . . _____

_____

. . . _____

_____

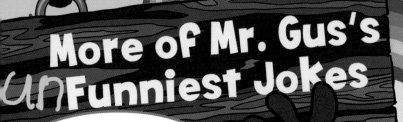

More of Mr. Gus's unFunniest Jokes

I FOUND A FEW MORE JOKES THAT WILL PROVE TO EVERYONE THAT I AM A NATURAL COMEDIAN.

IT'S OKAY IF YOU'RE NOT FUNNY.

BUT I AM FUNNY. ASK ME IF I'M A BANANA.

OKAY. ARE YOU A BANANA?

NO, I'M A DINOSAUR.

What's big, white, and can't climb a tree?
A refrigerator.

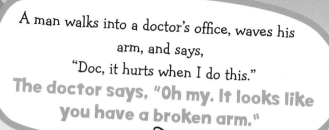

What do you call an orange that's been painted blue?
A blue.

Why can't Uncle Grandpa take pictures with a man with a wooden leg?
Because Uncle Grandpa can only take pictures with a camera.

Why couldn't Belly Bag go into the men's room?

Because he's not a mailbag.

SO A TEACHER SAYS, "WHOEVER ANSWERS MY NEXT QUESTION CAN GO HOME." ONE BOY THROWS HIS BACKPACK OUT THE WINDOW. THE TEACHER ASKS, "WHO JUST THREW THAT?"

THE BOY SHOUTS, "ME! CAN I GO HOME NOW?"

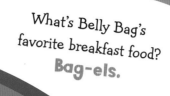

What's Belly Bag's favorite breakfast food? **Bag-els.**

What do you call a sleeping Belly Bag? **A nap sack.**

OKAY, I'VE FOUND SOME MORE JOKES. THEY'RE GUARANTEED TO MAKE ANYONE LAUGH.

Uncle Grandpa's Funniest Jokes Part 3

I'M READY.

WHAT KIND OF SHOES DO NINJAS WEAR? SNEAKERS!

Did you hear about Mr. Gus's new corduroy pillows? They're making headlines.

Why did Uncle Grandpa invite the mushroom to his party?
Because he was a fungi to be with.

What did the Giant Realistic Flying Lion say when it was eating a clown?
This tastes funny to me.

99

What's worse than finding a worm in your apple?
Finding half a worm.

What makes the Leaning Tower of Pisa lean?
It never eats.

What building has the most stories?
The library.

100

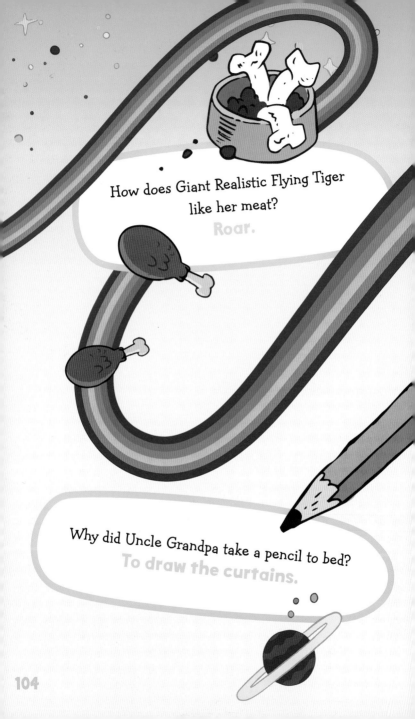

How does Giant Realistic Flying Tiger like her meat?

Roar.

Why did Uncle Grandpa take a pencil to bed?

To draw the curtains.

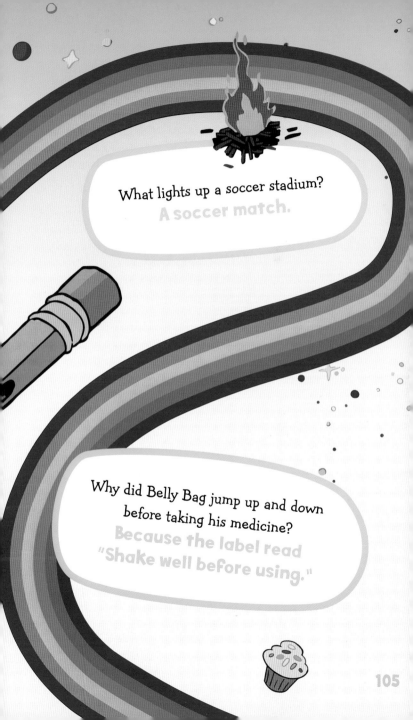

What lights up a soccer stadium?

A soccer match.

Why did Belly Bag jump up and down before taking his medicine?

Because the label read "Shake well before using."

How much does it cost a pirate to get earrings?

A buccaneer.

What is a zombie's least favorite room in the house?

The living room.

Why did the echo get detention at school?

For talking back.

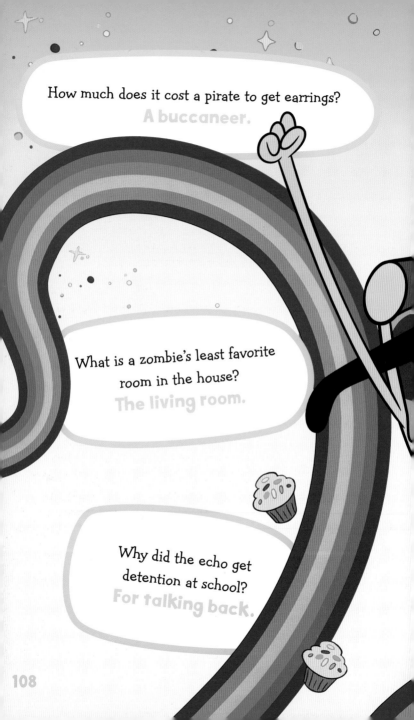

I THINK MY FAVORITE PARTS OF THE SHOW ARE THE SHORTS.

Uncle Grandpa's Short Jokes

YOU DON'T WEAR SHORTS.

I MEAN THE SHORT LITTLE CLIPS BETWEEN THE LONGER ONES. SO HERE ARE SOME VERY, VERY SHORT JOKES.

I went to an emotional wedding. Even the cake was in tiers.

Dry-erase boards are re-markable.

Exaggerations went up by a million percent last year.

I wrote a ballad about a tortilla. Well, actually, it's more of a wrap.

If olive oil comes from olives, where does baby oil come from?

How can you tell when you run out of invisible ink?

If a cow laughs, does milk come out of its nose?

What does cheese say when it poses for pictures?

How do you throw away a garbage can?

If you have a bunch of odds and ends, and you get rid of everything but just one, what do you call it?

What's another word for *synonym*?

115

And why . . .

. . . do you park in a driveway, and drive on a parkway?

. . . are boxing rings square?

. . . are feet smelly, and noses runny?

. . . is *abbreviation* such a long word?

The Joke's on Gus

MR. GUS STEPPED OUT, SO I'M GOING TO LAY ON YOU THE BEST DINOSAUR JOKES IN THE ENTIRE UNIVERSE. THEY WON THE, UM, BEST DINOSAUR JOKES IN THE ENTIRE UNIVERSE AWARDS LAST YEAR.

I'VE NEVER HEARD OF THOSE AWARDS.

THEY'RE VERY PRESTIGIOUS. IN FACT, THEY WERE HOSTED BY A PRESTIGIOUS-SAUR.

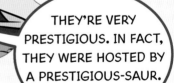

How do you make a dinosaur float? **With lots and lots of root beer and ice cream.**

120

Why do dinosaurs wear sandals?
So they don't sink in the sand.

Why do ostriches stick
their heads in the sand?
**To look for the dinosaurs that
forgot to wear their sandals.**

How do you get a dinosaur
on top of an oak tree?
**Put it on an acorn,
and wait fifty years.**

What if you don't want to wait fifty years?
Parachute it from an airplane.

Why isn't it safe to climb
oak trees between two and
four o'clock in the afternoon?
**Because that's when dinosaurs
practice their parachuting.**

125

This book almost has enough jokes in it, but we need a few more from you. Write your favorite jokes that you and your friends like to tell one another in the blanks provided below.

128